An opinio

T0102321

HISTORIC LONDON

Written by
SHELDON K. GOODMAN

Highgate Cemetery (no.22)

INFORMATION IS DEAD. LONG LIVE OPINION.

The idea of using a guidebook is rather historic, isn't it? Everything you could want can be downloaded from ChatGPT, surely.

No! This is a highly opinionated book: it's full of human, personal taste and, most crucially, it cuts through the dull stuff to reveal the gems. I'm ashamed to say history has always been dull to me. Until I went to Hampton Court (snooze) with my kids and touched Henry's tapestry (probably shouldn't have) and I had an epiphany: it's alive! It's here! And all this crazy, dirty, bloody, exciting stuff happened in London. It's waiting for you. In here. Out there. Go! Martin @ HMP

Other opinionated guides:

East London	*Escape London*
London Architecture	*Eco London*
Vegan London	*Big Kids' London*
London Green Spaces	*Art London*
Independent London	*Free London*
London Pubs	*Queer London*
Sweet London	*London Delis*
Kids' London	*London Hotels*

(This page) James Smith & Sons (no.2)
(Opposite) Leighton House (no.46)

The Hunterian Museum (no.3)

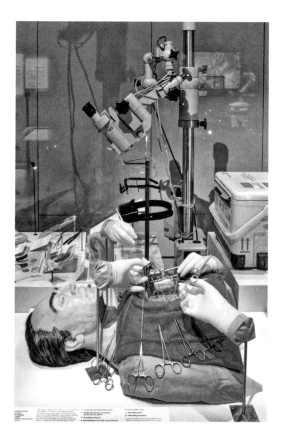

(This page) The Hunterian Museum (no.3)
(Opposite) Attendant (no.53)

Linley Sambourne's House (no.54)

NOT ALL HISTORY IS
IN GLASS CASES

London can be an overwhelming city, with so much to see and so much monumental history concentrated in one place. Founded by the Romans in 50CE, nearly two thousand years of culture, politics and power have shaped the capital, and, like peeling back the layers of an onion, there are myriad stories to uncover and historical clues to decipher. 'When a man is tired of London, he is tired of life,' said one of London's foremost wordsmiths, Samuel Johnson (no.11), in 1777. 'For there is in London all that life can afford.' This is no less true today, and to walk around London is to unravel the story of Britain, its people and its past.

This is by no means an exhaustive list of all the historic highlights of the capital: indeed, no book has ever been published that encompasses them all. But these are my personal (and opinionated) favourites, garnered from the decade I've spent as a walking tour guide in the city. There is so much more to the history of London than dusty museums. Some destinations I have discovered by accident while walking off the beaten path, such as Pickering Place (no.49), an intriguing den of iniquity, while others are must-see destinations you may be aware of, but don't really know that much about.

You will discover a city of contrasts, where regal splendour rubs shoulders with the stories of everyday people; from the Royal Opera House (no.18) to Wilton's Music Hall (no.25), and from the opulence of Greenwich's Painted Hall (no.35) to a facsimile of 19th-century docklands (no.27). Find out about curiously matched historical neighbours and the very different lives they led, two centuries apart, at the Handel Hendrix House (no.52), and witness the decadent architectural mash-up that is Eltham Palace (no.33), home to affluent socialites who grafted ostentatious contemporary design onto the remains of a Tudor palace.

If you find yourself in need of refreshment, stop off at one of London's historic pubs, such as The Black Friar (no.5), the capital's first theme pub (from 1905), or the Prospect of Whitby (no.28), where smugglers were hanged just downriver; or take a comfort break at the kooky and bijou coffee bar Attendant (no.53), formerly an ornate Victorian public lavatory. And if you want to dine like a king, head to Rules in Covent Garden (no.7), which is supposedly London's oldest restaurant, where royalty and celebrities alike have indulged in private affairs over game pie and Jersey rock oysters.

Step back in time and witness historic London first hand. Some of the entries are worthy of an entire day out, such as Hampton Court (no.36), while others, like the curious medical specimen-filled Hunterian Museum (no.3) and Sir John Soane's Museum (no.8) can be packaged up in one outing. You'll also find some suggested themed walks to enjoy. Although the city is in a perpetual state of change, its spirit across the centuries feels reassuringly familiar, and history is lurking surprisingly close to the surface – if you know where to look.

Sheldon K. Goodman, London 2023

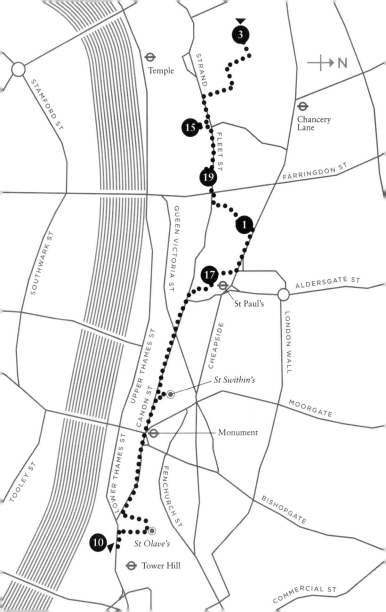

Temple

Chancery
Lane

STAMFORD ST

STRAND

FLEET ST

FARRINGDON ST

15

19

1

17

QUEEN VICTORIA ST

St Paul's

ALDERSGATE ST

LONDON WALL

SOUTHWARK ST

CHEAPSIDE

MOORGATE

UPPER THAMES ST

CANON ST

St Swithin's

Monument

TOWER THAMES ST

FENCHURCH ST

BISHOPGATE

TOOLEY ST

10

St Olave's

Tower Hill

COMMERCIAL ST

N

WALK 1

A deathly stroll through sites of
morbid curiosity, tragedy and tribute

Start at the *Hunterian Museum* **3**, examining gruesome specimens from the patients of an 18th-century surgeon. Make your way to the Strand and *Temple Church* **15**, from where the Knights Templar began their bloody crusades, then down Fleet Street to the creepy crypt of *St Bride's Church* **19**, with its iron casket (used to deter grave robbers). Continue down Ludgate Hill towards *The Old Bailey* **1**, built on the site of Newgate Prison – London's most feared jail and a place of public execution until 1868, then on to *St Paul's Cathedral* **17** to see the graves of Nelson, Wellington and Sir Christopher Wren. Head down Cannon Street to the former churchyard of *St Swithin's** to visit the memorial to Catrin Glyndŵr, daughter of Welsh freedom fighter Owain Glyndŵr, dedicated to the suffering of all women in war. Take a 15-minute walk to *St Olave's** to see the macabre trio of skulls above the doorway to the churchyard, and finish at the *Tower of London* **10**, with its long and grisly history of tragedy and death.

Walking time: 1.5 hours, 3.6 miles
Total time with stops: 4–5 hours
*Not in guidebook: more info online

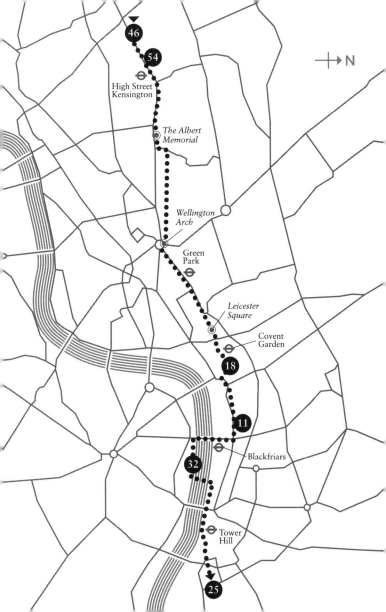

N

46

54

High Street
Kensington

*The Albert
Memorial*

*Wellington
Arch*

Green
Park

*Leicester
Square*

Covent
Garden

18

11

32

Blackfriars

Tower
Hill

25

WALK 2

*Whistlestop tour taking in highlights
of the city's artistic and literary heritage*

Begin at *Leighton House* **46**, ornate home of artist Lord Leighton. Proceed to High Street Kensington and turn down Phillimore Gardens to see *Punch* illustrator *Linley Sambourne's House* **54**. Head to Kensington Gardens to see *The Albert Memorial**, with its frieze depicting 169 celebrated artists, sculptors, composers, architects and poets. Continue to Hyde Park Corner and the *Wellington Arch**, which is hollow inside and houses an art gallery. Then veer towards Piccadilly to *Leicester Square**, where a statue to William Shakespeare watches over the tourists, and on towards Covent Garden to see the *Royal Opera House* **18**, home to British opera since 1732. Make your way through Aldwych and the Strand to *Dr Johnson's House* **11**, where the first English dictionary was written. Walk over Blackfriars Bridge and along the South Bank to see Shakespeare's *Globe Theatre* **32**. Finish by crossing Southwark Bridge and visiting *Wilton's Music Hall* **25**, the oldest surviving venue of its kind in the world.

*Walking time: 2.5–3 hours, 7.3 miles
Total time with stops: 6–7 hours
Not in guidebook: more info online

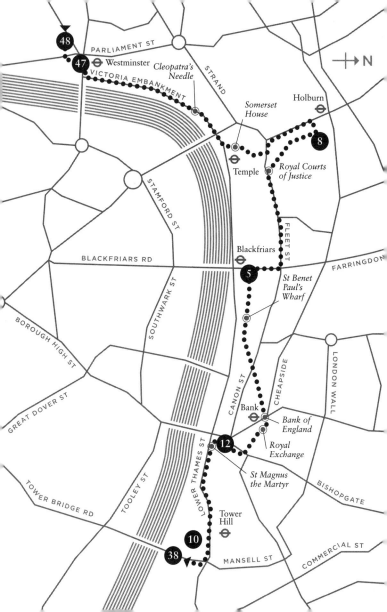

N

48

47 ⊖ Westminster

PARLIAMENT ST

VICTORIA EMBANKMENT

Cleopatra's Needle

STRAND

Somerset House

Holburn ⊖

8

⊖ Temple

Royal Courts of Justice

STAMFORD ST

FLEET ST

BLACKFRIARS RD

Blackfriars ⊖

5

FARRINGDON

SOUTHWARK ST

St Benet Paul's Wharf

BOROUGH HIGH ST

CANON ST

CHEAPSIDE

LONDON WALL

Bank ⊖

Bank of England

GREAT DOVER ST

12

Royal Exchange

BISHOPGATE

LOWER THAMES ST

St Magnus the Martyr

TOOLEY ST

Tower Hill ⊖

TOWER BRIDGE RD

10

38

MANSELL ST

COMMERCIAL ST

WALK 3

*A journey across 800 years
of the capital's architectural history*

Begin at the gothic 13th-century *Westminster Abbey* **48** then
cross over to Pugin and Barry's masterpiece, the *Palace of
Westminster* **47**. Stroll down Thames Embankment, taking
in *Cleopatra's Needle**, continue past *Somerset House**, a
neoclassical palace by Sir William Chambers, and head into
Lincoln's Inn, where the *Sir John Soane's Museum* **8** stands
out from its Georgian terrace. Admire the classical *Royal
Courts of Justice** on the Strand, before quenching your thirst
after a 15-minute walk to *The Black Friar* **5**, with sculpture by
Henry Poole and Nathaniel Hitch. Follow White Lion Hill to
the Dutch-influenced *St Benet Paul's Wharf** and Wren's well-
preserved Welsh Church. Walk to Bank, where William Tite's
Royal Exchange* stands alongside the *Bank of England**,
substantially rebuilt from Soane's original. Head down to
The Monument **12**, and at the bottom of Fish Street Hill see
St Magnus the Martyr*, which once opened onto the first
London Bridge and has a model of it inside. Finish by walking
down Lower Thames Street to *Tower Bridge* **38**, built to emu-
late the architecture of the *Tower of London* **10** next door.

Walking time: 1.5 hours, 4.2 miles
Total time with stops: 5–6 hours
*Not in guidebook: more info online

1

THE OLD BAILEY

Witness live courtroom drama

The country's most famous criminal court has
seen some of its most infamous trials, from Oscar
Wilde to the Krays. The notorious Newgate Prison
once stood here, and until 1868 Londoners flocked
to see the condemned hanged in a macabre car-
nival atmosphere. The grand marble interior of
this palace of justice rivals anything you'd see in
St Paul's Cathedral (17), and truly inspires a sense
of awe in the law. You can turn up on any week-
day and queue for entry to the public galleries, as
long as you dress appropriately and have ID (no
under 14s are permitted, and those under 16 must
be accompanied). Check online for a listing of
the day's cases – you may just get to witness legal
history in the making.

Old Bailey, EC4M 7EH
Nearest stations: St Paul's, City Thameslink
old-bailey.com

2

JAMES SMITH & SONS

London's last umbrella maker

A slice of Victoriana on New Oxford Street, London's historic brolly shop has stood virtually unchanged inside and out since the 1850s. With its 19th-century signage and polished brass exterior it is conspicuous among the parade of 21st-century shopfronts (it was the only one on the street to survive the Blitz). Inside, look out for the lucky horseshoes, here to ward against the bad luck of opening an umbrella indoors. This wet-weather emporium prides itself on selling bespoke umbrellas, canes and walking sticks (although dagger canes and swordsticks are no longer produced). These are custom made to the height of the user, and carry a lifetime warranty for repair in the on-site workshop. Your author owns an umbrella from here (with redwood crook) and can confirm it was built to last.

Hazlewood House, 513 New Oxford Street, WC1A 1BL
Nearest station: Tottenham Court Road
james-smith.co.uk

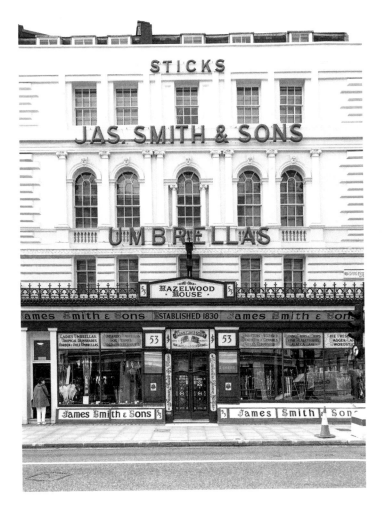

3

THE HUNTERIAN MUSEUM

The one with the thoroughly weird stuff in jars

This intriguing museum showcases the collection of 18th-century Scottish surgeon John Hunter, alongside displays examining the history of anatomy and surgery. In the somewhat claustrophobic galleries you'll discover dissected animals in jars and a grimly fascinating array of medical specimens, from foetuses to diseased limbs preserved in formaldehyde. Case studies of some of the people Hunter treated (including a former Prime Minister) add a human context to his gruesome practices. The museum today has addressed the contentious issue of displaying human remains by removing some of its previous displays, although the bones of Jonathan Wild, a notorious villain of London's underworld, remain.

Royal College of Surgeons of England,
38–43 Lincoln's Inn Fields, WC2A 3PE
Nearest station: Holborn
hunterianmuseum.org

4

ST BARTHOLOMEW'S HOSPITAL MUSEUM

900 years of medical history

Founded by a charitable 12th-century monk who believed that healthcare should be available to all, St Barts is still a functioning hospital. Above the entrance is the only statue to Henry VIII in London, erected to thank the King after he spared the hospital during his dissolution of the monasteries. The museum is to the north of the 18th-century central square, and inside you're confronted with nine centuries of medical history: grisly saws and surgical implements, specimens and rudimentary prosthetics in an array of cases and cabinets. On select days the wondrous staircase, which feels airlifted in from a stately home with its backdrop of floor-to-ceiling Hogarth paintings, is open and you can climb to the palatial Great Hall.

North Wing, St Bartholomew's Hospital,
West Smithfield, EC1A 7BE
Nearest station: City Thameslink
bartshealth.nhs.uk/bartsmuseum

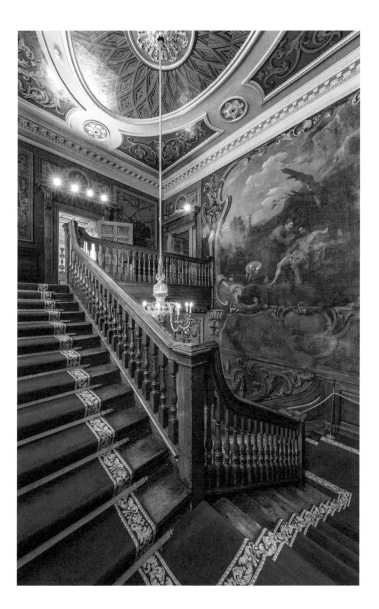

5

THE BLACK FRIAR

London's original theme pub – from 1905

Whether or not you're a fan of theme pubs, this one is well worth a visit: it is London's first, its extravagant and eccentric interior created at the turn of the century. Architect Herbert Fuller-Clark (whose music-hall designer father clearly had an influence on him) playfully acknowledged the Dominican friars who lived, worshipped and supped on this site from 1276 until 1539. The unassuming exterior belies the divine decor within, and you'd be forgiven for thinking you've wandered into a rather ornate church with a dazzling display of mosaics, reliefs and sculptures by notable artists of the era – including Henry Poole, who designed the famous HSBC Lions in Shanghai – along with stained glass and proverbs affixed to the walls. Bag yourself a booth and enjoy your history washed down with a pint.

174 Queen Victoria Street, EC4V 4EG
Nearest station: Blackfriars
@blackfriarpub

6

THE POSTAL MUSEUM

Delivering first-class fun by mail rail

A museum about the postal service may not immediately spark your interest, but trust us when we tell you that this is an unmissable experience. The superb Mail Rail utilises the narrow-gauge railway that once transported the post underground, and the old delivery platforms have become stages and soundscapes for one of London's more unusual rides. Sitting two-by-two in little trains only three carriages along, you can imagine yourself a parcel that's being delivered (if you so wish). The museum showcases postal history in galleries plastered with vintage adverts and signage, and periodically they open up the old tunnels so you can don a hard hat and follow the path of London's historic mail. An unexpectedly great place to visit.

15–20 Phoenix Place, WC1X 0DA
Nearest station: Farringdon
Paid entry
postalmuseum.org

7

RULES

Pull up a chair in this historic restaurant

Rules professes to be London's oldest restaurant, opening as an oyster bar in 1798. The interior has barely changed under three owners over two centuries: treacly mahogany panelling, plush velvet, and walls covered in caricatures from *Punch* contribute to the feeling that you're in an 18th-century private members club. All of the great and good of London have dined here, and, being surrounded by theatres, it has long been a haunt of thespians. Edward VII would entertain his mistress Lillie Langtry in Rules, and you too can eat like a king from a traditional British menu featuring plenty of game during the season (it's not the best choice for vegetarians). This may not be the cheapest meal in town, but it's worth it to feel so immersed in London's history – and for the very fancy doormen.

34–35 Maiden Lane, WC2E 7LB
Nearest stations: Covent Garden, Charing Cross
rules.co.uk

8

SIR JOHN SOANE'S MUSEUM

An architect's treasure-trove

The formidable architect, whose major works include the first Bank of England, was a hoarder of antiquity, turning his house into an archive stuffed to the rafters. Eventually his collection overflowed into neighbouring properties, and it's this mass of paintings, drawings and sculptures that survives in one of London's most eclectic and visually overwhelming museums (there are 40,000 objects, including a terrifyingly huge sarcophagus from the tomb of Egyptian Pharaoh Seti I). The museum hosts a range of events with free guided tours as well as 'Soane Lates', where you can see the classical sculptures by candlelight once a month. Avoid arriving with cumbersome bags as space is tight and you could accidentally damage priceless art.

13 Lincoln's Inn Fields, WC2A 3BP
Nearest station: Holborn
soane.org

9

GUILDHALL

Gruesome ancient history and world-class art

Most of the modern functions of the City of London Corporation are now based in newer buildings to the rear, which allows some of the older, most interesting parts of this cathedral of civic affairs to open up to visitors. The Guildhall Art Gallery is just off the enormous medieval Great Hall, where numerous state occasions have taken place over centuries, and houses over 250 masterpieces. You can gaze upon sublime art by John Everett Millais and the Pre-Raphaelites, before descending into the bowels of the building where you're confronted with the remains of a Roman amphitheatre from 70AD – a place of gladiatorial combat and public executions. You'll also find brilliant displays of artefacts representing nearly 2000 years of London history.

Gresham Street, EC2V 7HH
Nearest stations: Bank, Moorgate, St Paul's
guildhall.cityoflondon.gov.uk

10

THE TOWER OF LONDON

Birds, Beefeaters and bling

One of London's most recognisable landmarks, this has been a place of intrigue with a gory reputation since the 11th century. The Yeoman Warders offer theatrical tours that reveal the Tower's history, from royal menagerie to place of execution (as recently as the 20th century). The infamous ravens – who, legend has it, will cause the Tower to fall should they ever leave – have actually only been here since the 19th century, but the Crown Jewels have been under armed guard since 1661 and can be viewed via a travelator (to keep the awe-struck crowds moving) in a darkened gallery. Don't miss the daily Ceremony of the Keys, one of the oldest rituals of its kind and unchanged for 700 years (this is on a separate ticket and costs a fiver).

The Tower of London, EC3N 4AB
Nearest station: Tower Hill
Paid entry
hrp.org.uk/tower-of-london

11
DR JOHNSON'S HOUSE
The dictionary definition of literary history

Mind your language when you step into the Queen
Anne townhouse where Samuel Johnson wrote his
famous dictionary between 1748 and 1755. The
house was saved from dereliction by MP Cecil
Harmsworth in 1911, who insisted it be preserved
more like a home than a museum (you have to ring
the bell to enter) and welcomed tea parties to offset
the stuffiness you usually get with such places –
a practice the museum encourages to this day.
The front door still has its original anti-burglary
devices in place – a heavy chain and corkscrew
latch with a spiked fanlight – and the rest of the
house is decorated in period style with authentic
partitions and furnishings, evoking the era when
one of England's pre-eminent wordsmiths first put
pen to paper to record the English language.

17 Gough Square, EC4A 3DE
Nearest stations: Chancery Lane, City Thameslink
Paid entry
drjohnsonshouse.org

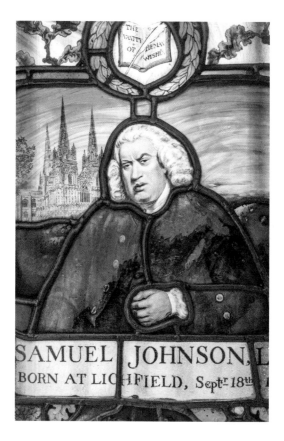

SAMUEL JOHNSON, L
BORN AT LICHFIELD, Septr 18th

Francis Greg

THE PLAN OF A DICTIONARY OF THE ENGLISH LANGUAGE

Addreſſed to the Right Honourable

PHILIP DOR

Earl of CHESTE

One of His MAJEST

12

THE MONUMENT

Oldest ticketed attraction with the best views

Although the Shard and Sky Garden offer higher vistas (and have accessibility built into the design), if you want a centuries-old bird's-eye view of London, go to the Monument. Built by Sir Christopher Wren and Robert Hooke to immortalise the Great Fire of 1666, it was originally intended to double as a laboratory-cum-telescope but its position in a busy city made this impossible. Be careful if you are claustrophobic: a narrow spiral staircase of 311 steps leads you 202 feet into the sky, with views as far as the Kent hills to the south and the upper ridge of Camden to the north. Check out historical graffiti scrawled on the walls, and cherish the little certificate you get for visiting this monument to a disaster that nearly razed the city.

Fish Street Hill, EC3R 8AH
Nearest station: Monument
Paid entry
themonument.org.uk

13
CHARLES DICKENS MUSEUM

Home to the great writer's legacy

The capital's most celebrated chronicler penned *Oliver Twist* and *Nicholas Nickleby* while living here. It's not hard to imagine how it was back then as this museum painstakingly recreates each room of his former home, from the chintzy blue and gold decor of the dining room to the sedate study where he conjured his colourful characters – containing the original desk on which he wrote *Great Expectations* and *A Tale of Two Cities*. Upstairs you can see Dickens' only surviving items of clothing, a dinner suit he wore in 1870, surprisingly small for such a giant of literature. In the garden is the headstone of the illustrator Robert Seymour, regarded as being responsible for his first literary success but whom Dickens refused to credit.

48–49 Doughty Street, WC1N 2LX
Nearest station: Russell Square
Paid entry
dickensmuseum.com

14

FOUNDLING MUSEUM

Heartbreaking history of London's at-risk children

This museum tells the stories of children abandoned at the Foundling Hospital, started by philanthropist Thomas Coram in 1739, juxtaposed against those who find themselves in care today. Among the more tragic objects on display are the individual tokens that mothers left with their children – everyday items including coins, bracelets and buttons – in the hope that one day these could be used to identify and return their child. Sadly, in most cases this didn't happen. The museum contains one of the finest examples of rococo architecture in London, the Court Room, which houses an art collection – with pieces donated by William Hogarth and Benjamin West – displayed exactly as it was in the 18th century, when it was used to raise funds for the hospital.

40 Brunswick Square, WC1N 1AZ
Nearest station: Russell Square
Paid entry
foundlingmuseum.org.uk

15
TEMPLE CHURCH

London's Jerusalem, home of the Knights Templar

Situated in the heart of London's legal quarter, Temple Church was founded in 1119 by an order of crusading monks, and numerous historically significant events have taken place here over the centuries (it's where the Magna Carta was outlined, and the basis for American law first established). Modelled on the Church of the Holy Sepulchre in Jerusalem, you'll doubtless recognise it from its many TV and film appearances, notably as a location in *The Da Vinci Code*. The entrance is majestic, with columns surrounding the West Doorway topped by four carved busts, some wearing turbans – a troubling nod to the Knights' foes in their holy crusades. To best experience the church, go to one of the truly transcendent choral performances that are regularly held here.

Temple, EC4Y 7BB
Nearest station: Temple
Paid entry
templechurch.com

16

ST DUNSTAN IN THE EAST

Plants are the new religion in this open-air church

The church was rebuilt many times since its foundation in the 12th century, but Sir Christopher Wren's final iteration ultimately became one of the many casualties of the Blitz. Fortunately for us, it was decided to retain the ruins as a public garden, and its ivy-draped walls are one of the most beguiling sights in London. The gardeners challenge themselves to ensure something is in flower 365 days of the year, and the nave is lush with mature trees and shrubbery – in stark contrast to the jumbled office blocks that surround it. A gentle fountain provides a serene soundtrack for those who want to take a contemplative step away from the hubbub of the City – or simply eat a sandwich in peace.

St Dunstan's Hill, EC3R 5DD
Nearest station: Monument
cityoflondon.gov.uk/st-dunstan-in-the-east-church-garden

17

ST PAUL'S CATHEDRAL

A truly spiritual experience in the Square Mile

Ascending the stone steps of the grand west entrance you can't help but feel intimidated by the looming ostentatiousness of Sir Christopher Wren's masterpiece. Enormous elephant's leg-like marble pillars uphold the classical interior, with frescoes that make you feel as if you are in a celestial space. Visit the crypt to see the tombs of some of England's finest military, literary, architectural and musical heroes, including Wren himself. If you can bear heights, take a trip up past the Whispering Gallery to the top of the dome: it's like scaling a mountain via narrow service ducts. It's free to worship here, and some of the concerts and performances – such as the Sunday organ concert – are too, but paid guided tours are offered as well as ticketed late-night special events.

St Paul's Churchyard, EC4M 8AD
Nearest station: St Paul's
Paid entry
stpauls.co.uk

18

ROYAL OPERA HOUSE

Historic home to the high arts

Tucked away in the colonnades of Covent Garden, this is the third theatre on this site, the others having burned down. It opened its doors in 1858, and became home to the Royal Ballet. There's more to see and do here than attend the (often eye-wateringly expensive) shows. The gift shop is a gallery of prints of former performances, and the main entrance foyer showcases costumes from famous productions (with some also on the first floor), with displays changing every six months or so. Take the escalator to the rooftop bar and you'll see the magnificent Floral Hall, which was inspired by the Crystal Palace; it was originally built to house a flower market but became a venue for night-time performances, and here you can see free lunchtime recitals and rehearsals on Fridays.

Bow Street, WC2E 9DD
Nearest station: Covent Garden
roh.org.uk

19

ST BRIDE'S CHURCH

Layers of history beneath the journalists' church

The 226 ft-tall steeple of St Bride's is said to have inspired the design of the tiered wedding cake in the late 18th century, when a baker in nearby Ludgate Hill looked at the second tallest spire in the City and revolutionised the matrimonial sweet treat forever. Designed by Sir Christopher Wren, St Bride's saw much post-war refurbishment, largely financed by the newspapers who once dominated the surrounding streets. In the corner of the church there is a memorial dedicated to journalists who have died in the line of duty. Don't miss the crypt, where you can see the church through the ages, including pieces of Roman pavement, fragments of a church bell and an iron coffin that was designed to deter body snatchers.

Fleet Street, EC4Y 8AU
Nearest station: City Thameslink
stbrides.com

20

THE BRITISH MUSEUM

A world of history across 990,000 square feet

Housing ancient ephemera for nearly three centuries and sprawling over three floors, you could spend a week here and still not see everything. Once a repository for loot from the empire, the museum has taken pains to redress its colonial past and present accurate histories of its collections. Visitors are drawn to headliners like the Rosetta Stone, the medieval Lewis Chessmen and the Easter Island Statue, but there are many other wonders to discover – from the Sutton Hoo treasures that whisper of life in Anglo Saxon England to a figure of the Indian goddess Kali, whose mouth inspired the Rolling Stones' logo. Avoid the temptation to make a beeline for Egypt and check out the stately tomb guardians of General Liu Tingxun in the often-overlooked India and China galleries at the back of the museum.

Great Russell Street, WC1B 3DG
Nearest station: Tottenham Court Road
britishmuseum.org

21

ISOKON BUILDING

Suspense meets style in a modernist masterpiece

Today it's best known as the place where 'queen of crime' Agatha Christie lived and wrote some of her best-known works. But this Grade 1 listed building was also the very first modernist block in London, a 1930s experiment in minimalist design, which attracted artists, spies and bohemians – including founder of the Bauhaus, Walter Gropius. The former garage has now been converted into a permanent exhibition space which, although small, packs a punch: you can see original Isokon furniture by designers including Gropius and Marcel Breuer alongside displays exploring the lasting legacy of Christie and her characters, and some highlighting the exploits of former staff – such as the first TV celebrity chef Philip Harben, who ran the kitchens of the building in the late 1930s.

Isokon Gallery, Lawn Road, NW3 2XD
Nearest station: Belsize Park
isokongallery.org

22

HIGHGATE CEMETERY

London's best-known Victorian Valhalla

It's not the biggest or oldest of London's cemeteries, but it is the most famous, opened in the mid-19th century along with Tower Hamlets (no.30) and five others to accommodate the city's dead. Spectacular circular catacombs are prime deathly real estate where dynasties could be laid to rest – now home to rare species of spider and bat. Many illustrious Londoners lie in this leafy labyrinth, most famously Karl Marx, alongside numerous artistic and literary heavyweights and titans of industry, with George Michael and Beryl Bainbridge being more recent internments. A peaceful and inspiring spot to wander and ponder the transience of life, both sides of the cemetery are now open for guided or self-guided tours.

Swain's Lane, N6 6PJ
Nearest station: Archway
Paid entry
highgatecemetery.org

23

ST PANCRAS
NEW CHURCH

'New' church in an ancient parish

When it was built in the early 19th century, this was the biggest place of Christian worship to be erected in London since St Paul's, and was inspired by the Athenian Tower of Winds and the Erechtheion – both on the Acropolis in Greece. Rumour has it the figures that watch over the entrance to the burial vault were made too tall for their recesses so the sculptor had to remove sections of their waists to make them fit. Created as an auditorium as much as for worship, this is the home of the London Festival for Contemporary Church Music, held annually in May, and its crypt – built to hold 2000 bodies but very rarely used – is now an art gallery, the vaults becoming their own private creative spaces.

Euston Road, NW1 2BA
Nearest station: Euston
stpancraschurch.org

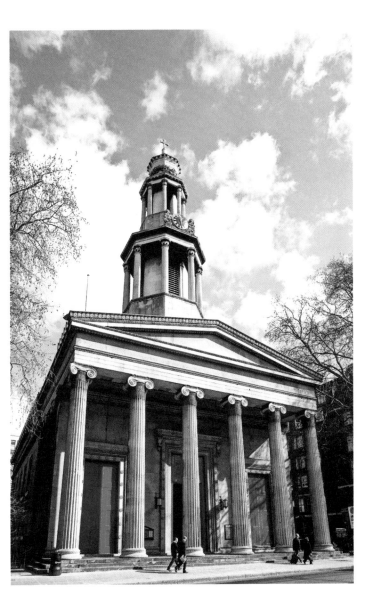

24

THE CANAL MUSEUM

History of what were once London's lifeblood

This hidden gem of a museum tells the story of London's canals, integral to the capital's success. The building has its own quirky story, originally built to store ice shipped from Norway by a Swiss-Italian restaurateur, Carlo Gatti, who helped popularise ice cream in Britain. In this former warehouse the fascinating history of London's waterways is revealed, from Roman times to the Olympic Park's regeneration of a polluted network of clogged canals. Step inside a 1930s narrowboat to explore what it was like transporting timber and steel before roads and railways took over, and take a boat ride along the Regent's Canal to the Islington Tunnel – occasionally as far as Little Venice and Victoria Park.

12–13 New Wharf Road, N1 9RT
Nearest station: King's Cross St Pancras
Paid entry
canalmuseum.org.uk

25
WILTON'S MUSIC HALL

The world's oldest surviving Grand Music Hall

You can almost still hear the raucous crowds in this battered venue. In the mid 19th-century, John Wilton decided to extend an existing pub and bring West End entertainment to the people of the East End, creating a gas-lit fun palace where famous performers such as George Leybourne and Madam Senyah once graced the stage. The distressed interior of rough brickwork, wooden panelling and flaking layers of paint offers clues as to the building's eclectic history as a Methodist Hall and rag warehouse, before it was rebooted as a music hall. Gone are the gaslights, but this intimate space evokes a long-lost era, and today you can see performances ranging from reimagined Gilbert and Sullivan to Shakespeare and cabaret – reviving old East End entertainment for the 21st century.

1 Graces Alley, E1 8JB
Nearest station: Shadwell
Paid entry for events
wiltons.org.uk

26

DENNIS SEVERS' HOUSE

Theatrical spin on a historic Huguenot home

This 18th-century building was bought in 1979 by Dennis Severs, a Californian artist who loved British history and wanted to restore the house to reflect how its original Huguenot silk weaver inhabitants lived. Each room is decorated in a different historical style, spanning three centuries of the fictional Jervis family, and is like walking through a monumental stage set: imagine Bridgerton, but with less historically accurate substitutes from local department stores adding to the fun-house feel. Severs was a wildly eccentric character who would throw infamous house parties and conduct guided tours with bizarre sound effects. These days, gentle soundtracks of creaking floorboards add to the atmospheric vibe.

18 Folgate Street, E1 6BX
Nearest station: Liverpool Street
Paid entry
dennissevershouse.co.uk

27

MUSEUM OF LONDON, DOCKLANDS

Empire, trade and Victoriana

This is a properly good local museum – one that is by, about and for Londoners. The exterior – ignoring the slick chain restaurants that flank it – gives a sense of the scale from the days when this was the epicentre of a different kind of trading industry, before finance moved in. Set over three floors of a former warehouse where timber and sugar were once unloaded, the museum presents an authentic account of docklands. Whistle an old music hall song as you explore the dark warren of Sailor Town, a recreated street network of the 19th-century docks complete with facsimiles of pubs and homes, or marvel at the quaffable quality of a bottle of beer salvaged from the *Princess Alice* river disaster of 1878.

No.1 Warehouse, West India Quay, E14 4AL
Nearest station: West India Quay
museumoflondon.org.uk/museum-london-docklands

28

PROSPECT OF WHITBY

Gallows humour in an old riverside hostelry

Trading as a public house since the 16th century, this is London's oldest riverside pub and a historic hangout in a quite literal sense. The veranda at the back gives an enviable view of the Thames, but the gallows on the foreshore hint at a much darker past, and are a wink to this being the favourite pub of notorious 'Hanging' Judge Jeffreys. This area was once an epicentre for smugglers and other ne'er-do-wells who met their end at Execution Dock, just downriver (where infamous Captain William Kidd, sea captain-turned-pirate, was hanged). In more recent history, this was also a haunt of both Frank Sinatra and Muhammad Ali. Inside, the original 400-year-old flagstone floor and a rare example of a pewter-topped bar remain.

57 Wapping Wall, E1W 3SH
Nearest station: Wapping
greeneking-pubs.co.uk/pubs/greater-london/
prospect-of-whitby

29
MUSEUM OF
THE HOME

Evolution of the home over four centuries

This museum not only presents intriguing snap-
shots of homes through time, but also encourages
you to question what *makes* a home, and takes
pains to represent those of a broad demographic.
Based in Sir Robert Geffrye's Almshouses, originally built for the widows of ironmongers in 1715,
the galleries are contained within the footprints of
the old dwellings. 400 years of domestic history are
on display here, and you can see recreations of a
cluttered 1870s parlour, an eye-popping orange and
brown 1970s living room and an industrial-chic
1990s loft apartment. There are nasty reminders
of household horrors like bed bugs and unsavoury
odours, and delightful grounds that track garden
design over the centuries.

136 Kingsland Road, E2 8EA
Nearest station: Hoxton
museumofthehome.org.uk

30

TOWER HAMLETS CEMETERY PARK

The people's graveyard

This is one of the 'Magnificent Seven', a ring of Victorian cemeteries that includes the famously grand Highgate (no.22), but unlike the bourgeoisie buried there, these folk led lives that are more relatable. The Blitz Memorial honours locals who lost their lives in air raids and is made of bricks from the bombed-out buildings. Look out for the tomb of Joseph Westwood, a shipbuilder whose employees founded what became West Ham FC, and the monument to 500 children from Dr Barnardo's orphanages, buried in unmarked graves here a century ago. Besides housing the dead, the park is a vital living space teeming with wildlife, and the Friends of Tower Hamlets Cemetery Park offer guided tours, bat walks and Forest Schools.

Southern Grove, E3 4PX
Nearest stations: Mile End, Bow Road
fothcp.org

31
THE BRUNEL MUSEUM

Architectural engineering that changed the world

This diminutive museum celebrates the first tunnel ever to be built beneath a river, and the dynasty that achieved this spectacular feat of 19th-century engineering. Artefacts and souvenirs from the tunnel's operation are displayed within the engine house, and the old tunnel shaft has recently been opened to visitors for the first time in 150 years, offering a glimpse of our industrial heritage. The museum explores often overlooked stories, including women associated with the site as well as its links to LGBTQ+ history, and there is a diverse calendar of events, from monthly classical concerts in the outdoor space to pop-up cocktail bars. Don't forget to pop over the road to the historic Mayflower pub, from where the Pilgrim Fathers are said to have set sail for America in 1620.

Railway Avenue, SE16 4LF
Nearest station: Rotherhithe
Paid entry
thebrunelmuseum.com

32

SHAKESPEARE'S GLOBE

(Sort-of) authentic copy of the 16th-century theatre

It's often said that you're not a proper actor if you haven't performed at the Globe, and I'd add that you're not a proper Londoner until you've seen a play here. The Globe is a combination of two previous incarnations of the original theatre, and utilises the same material (green oak) and historic building techniques. The thatched roof – which required special permission because of the fire risk – and ye olde design almost fool you into thinking it has survived from an earlier age, and you half expect the bard himself to saunter on stage. The open-air theatre has a range of seating, standing being the cheapest (if a bit severe on your ankles), and Shakespeare's back catalogue is in regular rotation along with more modern productions.

21 New Globe Walk, Bankside, SE1 9DT
Nearest station: Blackfriars
Paid entry
shakespearesglobe.com

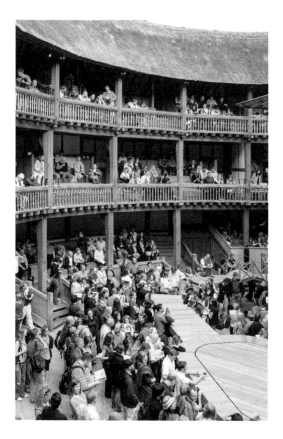

33

ELTHAM PALACE

Unique fusion of medieval and art deco

A former medieval and Tudor royal residence, the palace is probably better known for its ostentatious display of wealth and social standing, the decor designed for socialites Stephen and Virginia Courtauld in the 1930s. No expense was spared in creating beautiful interiors in exotic woods with bespoke marquetry, underfloor heating, pristine gardens, and accommodation for their pet ring-tailed lemur, Mah-Jongg. It is said that even the Queen Mother thought the decor was a bit a much. The Courtaulds' tastes are given free rein in the parts of the house they exclusively used – don't miss Virginia's glamorous onyx bathroom featuring gold mosaic and the statue of a Greek goddess. An extraordinary mash-up of medieval, Tudor and art deco that you simply won't see anywhere else.

Court Yard, SE9 5QE
Nearest station: Mottingham
english-heritage.org.uk/visit/places/
eltham-palace-and-gardens

34

HMS BELFAST

Retired warship with nine decks to explore

Permanently moored on The Queen's Walk in Southwark, HMS *Belfast*, built in the same ship-yard as RMS *Titanic*, saw action on D-Day and served in Asia and the Korean War before being retired from active service in 1963. This is more than just a battleship, it was a floating city complete with chapel, in-ship radio station and well-used galley kitchen, and there's tons to explore, from the captain's quarters to the engine room and gun turrets. In some parts it's a little claustrophobic and navigating your way through the ship requires climbing steep ladders up to various decks, par-ticularly if you want to see the artillery shells in the ship's bowels. You can also book for 'Kip in a Ship', where kids can have a sleepover in this legendary light cruiser.

The Queen's Walk, SE1 2JH
Nearest station: London Bridge
Paid entry
iwm.org.uk/visits/hms-belfast

35

THE PAINTED HALL

Spectacular oil painting across 40,000 square feet

Prepare to be wowed when you set eyes on the Painted Hall. Created from 1707–1726 by James Thornhill, it's said that two decades of painting Britain's equivalent to the Sistine Chapel forever ruined his back. He deployed tricks of the eye to make the hall seem more opulent than it really was – those columns aren't fluted, for example. Ceilings and walls are covered in paintings, some made to look like sculpture, featuring monarchs such as William and Mary and George I along with mythical characters. Handy mirrors and pouffes are provided so you can comfortably lay back and take it all in, and look out for the ghostly hand of a painted-over figure that is likely to have been George I's estranged wife Sophia on the West Wall.

Old Royal Naval College, Greenwich, SE10 9NN
Nearest station: Cutty Sark
Paid entry
ornc.org/explore-whats-here/painted-hall

36

HAMPTON COURT PALACE

Regal residence across the ages

You'll need to dedicate an entire day to see Hampton Court as there are three distinct eras of royal occupation to view. The smoky Great Kitchen of Tudor times, put to good use during the reign of the corpulent Henry VIII, still roasts meat from a roaring hearth at weekends; the Great Hall hosts historical re-enactments; and the more refined tapestry-filled private apartments of King William III give an insight into how the monarch lived. The grounds, from the elegant 17th-century Privy Garden to the famous maze, are great for exploring, but it's the opulent Chapel Royal with its blue and gold vaulted ceiling that is the highlight of the entire palace. This is a superb daytrip that's worth the slog to the far reaches of Zone 6.

Hampton Court Way, East Molesey, KT8 9AU
Nearest station: Hampton Court
Paid entry
hrp.org.uk/hampton-court-palace

37

OLD OPERATING THEATRE

A place of healing that's close to God

Climb the winding stone staircase to the top of the church of St Thomas' hospital, and concealed in the roof space you'll find the remains of an operating theatre and herb garret. The rafters were perfect for drying herbs used to treat the sick, and by the 1820s part of the space was converted for surgical use. This is the oldest antiseptic theatre in existence in the UK and has a spooky Hogwarts feel, with medical implements on display and skeletons in cabinets. It makes you thankful that the NHS now has a cleaner, more clinical approach. The theatre is naturally built for performance, and a regular roster of events includes demonstrations of Victorian surgical practices, medically themed stand-up comedy and puppet shows.

9a St Thomas Street, SE1 9RY
Nearest station: London Bridge
Paid entry
oldoperatingtheatre.com

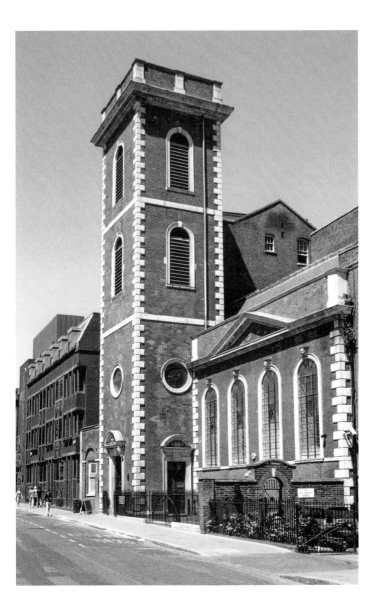

38
TOWER BRIDGE

Iconic landmark and feat of engineering

Officially this is the river entrance to the City of London, and its design was supposed to mimic its famous neighbour, the Tower of London – which is why it looks much older than its 130-odd years. Once inside, you can climb the wooden staircase all the way up to the high-level walkways, discovering the history of the bridge along the way. The summit offers unparalleled views of London upriver and down, and a massive glass floor panel allows you to stand and watch the traffic far below – not for the faint-hearted! Down in the bowels of the bridge are enormous bascule chambers – huge brick vaults that allow movement for the road bridge's counterweights every time it's opened – and you can visit the engine room to see the steam-powered engines once used to raise the bascules.

Tower Bridge Road, SE1 2UP
Nearest station: Tower Hill
Paid entry
towerbridge.org.uk

39

CROSSNESS PUMPING STATION

Ornate cathedral of sewage

It's almost as if the Victorians were so disgusted with the idea of a sewage station that they over-compensated by producing this masterpiece of Romanesque architecture. Built between 1859 and 1865, it was part of engineer Joseph Bazalgette's solution to 'de-stink' the city. It's been out of action since the 1950s, but much of the building has been restored, and one of its pumps, the Prince Consort, brought back to working order. Inside, the station is a dizzying display of vivid colours and patterns that has to be seen to be believed, resembling a Persian palace or a steampunk dream. You will need to pre-book your visit, and guided tours are available on certain days – and they positively encourage visits from photography clubs.

Bazalgette Way, Abbey Wood, SE2 9AQ
Nearest station: Abbey Wood
Paid entry
crossness.org.uk/visit.html

40

SHAD THAMES

Docklands past and present

Look skywards when walking through Shad Thames and you can easily imagine the rush of barrels or the hoisting of goods could start up at any moment. Now the stomping ground of the well-heeled, you don't need to go back too far to a time when the people who lived and worked in what was known as 'the larder of London' were far less fancily shod. Originally built as warehouses for the ships that once docked here, when the Port of London finally closed in the 1980s creatives moved in, and then the regeneration of Canary Wharf as a financial centre made it an estate agent's dream. Now many of the criss-crossing bridges are private gardens and walkways, and the streets are a nicer extension of the cafes and bars you find around London Bridge.

Shad Thames, SE1 2NW
Nearest station: London Bridge

41

DULWICH PICTURE GALLERY

The world's first public art gallery

Opened with great fanfare in 1817, the DPG was designed by Sir John Soane (no.8), who utilised innovative roof lanterns to make use of natural light to illuminate the galleries. Not many know that it is also a tomb, containing the bones of three of its founders who donated their collections. Tudor art hangs on jewel-coloured walls alongside paintings by Old Masters ranging from Canaletto to Rembrandt and Rubens, and Guido Reni's erotic and devotional picture of Saint Sebastian is of note for its early queer allegory. As well as the permanent collection there are rotating exhibitions and events, and the gallery boasts one of the loveliest museum grounds in all of London.

Gallery Road, SE21 7AD
Nearest station: West Dulwich
Paid entry
dulwichpicturegallery.org.uk

42

THE QUEEN'S HOUSE

Queens galore in Britain's first classical building

This stately home has certainly lived up to its name
in recent history. Every February it hosts an event
celebrating the site's queer history (both James I
and the later Queen Anne were rumoured to have
had same-sex relationships), with drag performers
and historians uniting to showcase queer libera-
tion and LGBTQ+ representation. The Queen's
House was the country's first classical building,
and houses a breathtaking art collection – including the famous 'Armada' portrait of Elizabeth I in
a voluminous dress and a ruff resembling a dinner
plate. Don't miss the Instagrammable Tulip Staircase, and in the Great Hall be sure to look up at the
ceiling, which was designed by Turner prize-winner
Richard Wright and mirrors the geometry of the
marble floor.

Romney Road, SE10 9NF
Nearest station: Cutty Sark
rmg.co.uk/queens-house

43

BLACK CULTURAL ARCHIVE

Only British institution dedicated to Black heritage

This important archive was founded in 1981 – at a time of incredible racism and hostility in Britain – by activist and historian Len Garrison, to give a home to African and Caribbean history. It opened on this site in Brixton in 2014, and houses artefacts ranging from an ancient silver coin featuring Black Roman Emperor Septimius Severus to the personal letters of composer Samuel Coleridge-Taylor. There are resources designed to educate about Black histories, struggles and achievements, and an online collection that is impressively catalogued. A rolling calendar of exhibitions examine the British Black experience – with previous ones looking at the history of the Rastafari Movement in Britain and the Windrush Generation.

1 Windrush Square, SW2 1EF
Nearest station: Brixton
Paid entry
blackculturalarchives.org

44

ROUPELL STREET

Perfectly preserved pocket of living history

Years of accumulated grime from nearby Waterloo station and the long-gone industry of the area has dirtied the bricks from yellow to brown, but this atmospheric street is instantly Instagrammable and a favourite of film and TV location scouts (you may recognise it as the Kray twins' home in *Legend,* and from *Doctor Who*). The former workers' cottages were built in the Georgian era by metal merchant and property magnate John Roupell, and often contained 20 people per household. Having survived the Blitz as well as the developers, its conservation status has ensured the street remains a time capsule of a working-class terrace. Some of the houses even still have small brass plaques attached – a relic from the days when this indicated if the house was insured against fire.

Roupell Street, SE1
Nearest station: Waterloo

45

KENSINGTON PALACE

Historic royal palace and gardens

Kensington Palace was the country residence of William and Mary in 1689 as well as the childhood home of Queen Victoria, although these days it's better known as where Princess Diana lived post-divorce. It's now the official London residence of her eldest son, and is under the guardianship of the Historic Royal Palaces. You might not be able to pop in on Prince William, but you can visit the historic apartments, including the room where Queen Victoria was told she'd be starting her long reign, the Jewel Room, featuring pieces commissioned for the monarch, and the impressive King's staircase, where warders guarded the private rooms of George I. A visit to the palace wouldn't be complete without a walk around, and a picnic in, the tranquil Kensington Gardens.

Kensington Gardens, W8 4PX
Nearest stations: High Street Kensington, Queensway
Paid entry
hrp.org.uk/kensington-palace

46

LEIGHTON HOUSE

The finest orientalist interior in London

Victorian artist Lord Frederic Leighton was not a man to conform, and the dreary chintz that filled many homes in the late 19th-century is absent here. The plain exterior opens into an extravagant palace of art, where Leighton set out to show how an artist should live. The house is filled with ceramics and textiles inspired by his travels: marvel at the Arab Hall, where walls are covered in intricate Islamic tiles, topped with a golden dome, and light filters through the mashrabiyya (wooden screens). This opulence is evident everywhere, from Leighton's dark-red studio to his silk-lined gallery. Check online for poetry readings, exhibitions and drawing classes held here, and if you're low on cash time your visit for the first Monday of the month, when you can pay whatever entrance fee you can afford.

12 Holland Park Road, W14 8LZ
Nearest station: High Street Kensington
Paid entry
rbkc.gov.uk/museums

47

THE PALACE OF WESTMINSTER

Walk the corridors of power

This gothic wonder began life as a royal residence centuries ago, but is now at the heart of British Government. It's currently undergoing a colossal refurbishment, which includes having Big Ben repainted to its original design and stripping out years of dodgy wiring. Parts of the building are open to the public – but be prepared for the security scrutiny. You can queue to watch sittings in the Houses of Commons and Lords (behind bullet-proof glass) as well as book tickets to see the Prime Minister trade barbs with the leader of the Opposition at Prime Minister's Question Time. The Speaker's apartments, featuring the enticingly named Crimson Drawing Room and the State Bedroom, are also on the paid public tour roster.

St Margaret Street, SW1A 0AA
Nearest station: Westminster
Paid entry for tours
parliament.uk

48
WESTMINSTER ABBEY

Vaulted and exalted royal church

Built in the 13th century in the historic heart of
Westminster, this majestic masterpiece is still the
epicentre of many public events. Aside from the
religious function of the building, it's also the rest-
ing place of many of London's great and good – a
bit like the Ivy, but more sepulchral. Numerous
mausoleums and tombs are cluttered inside, and
the recently refurbished Queen's Diamond Jubilee
Galleries contain wax effigies of former monarchs
(used in their funerals) displayed by the royal
tombs. The galleries also provide a breathtaking
view looking down the nave of the Abbey. If the
admission price is a bit too steep for your wallet,
slip round the side through Dean's Yard and head
for the entrance signposted Cellarium Cafe. You'll
be able to visit some parts of the Abbey for free.

20 Dean's Yard, SW1P 3PA
Nearest station: Westminster
Paid entry
westminster-abbey.org

49

PICKERING PLACE

Tiny square – with a big reputation

Next door to wine emporium Berry Bros. & Rudd (no.55) is a narrow passageway that leads to London's smallest square – the last place in England where a duel was fought. The alley is lined with dark wooden panels and lit by its original gaslight, and it's said that the secluded square was once a magnet for illicit activity, from terrible blood sports such as bear baiting to gambling and duels. From 1836–1845 it was the location of the Texas Legation, when Texas was an independent country before joining the USA, which is commemorated here on a gold plaque (Texas left an unpaid rent bill that wasn't settled until 1986). Stepping from the dark passage into the pretty Georgian square you truly feel transported back to the 18th century.

Pickering Place, off St James Street, SW1Y 5HZ
Nearest station: Green Park

50

CHURCHILL WAR ROOMS

Britain's wartime nerve centre

Hunker down in the underground command centre that was integral to the Allied victory in World War II. This top-secret space even had its own BBC studio during the war, to allow Winston Churchill to make speeches from there. It also serves as a memorial to the life of the cigar-chomping Prime Minister, and you can see the original No.10 Downing Street door that he walked through as well as exhibitions about his life and accounts of what he was like to work for. It's a strange feeling to walk in Churchill's footsteps through the subterranean corridors, and to look at his chair in the wartime bunker – which still bears the marks of his anxious clawing as he awaited updates from the field.

King Charles Street, SW1A 2AQ
Nearest station: Westminster
Paid entry
iwm.org.uk/visits/churchill-war-rooms

51

JAMES J. FOX

Old fashioned cigar merchant with a museum

Resembling an old curiosity shop, this is considered to be the world's oldest cigar shop. It dates back to the late 18th century, and is where Winston Churchill and Oscar Wilde bought their smokes. The first thing that hits you is the unmistakable aroma of roasted tobacco, and behind the counter are gold urns containing myriad blends, with pipes and cigar cutters deftly displayed in original glass cabinets. This is a shop that caters to true tobacco-aficionados, with walk-in humidors where cigars are stored for the likes of Harvey Keitel, and a sampling lounge that's one of the few places in London where you can smoke indoors. Downstairs is a fascinating museum where royal warrants and memorabilia from the shop's long history are on display, including the chair Churchill would sit in on his visits.

19 St James's Street, SW1A 1ES
Nearest station: Green Park
jjfox.co.uk

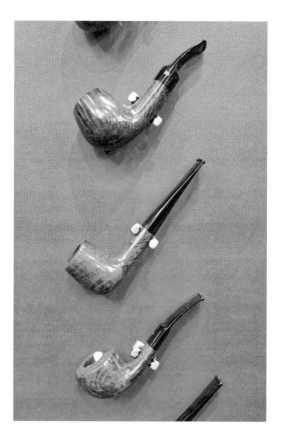

52

HANDEL
HENDRIX HOUSE

Musical memories from both ends of the scale

Two of the greatest musicians of all time were
neighbours – albeit two centuries apart – and have
a museum jointly dedicated to their very different lives and legacies. A Georgian townhouse that
Handel would have been familiar with has been
faithfully decorated, complete with wood-panelled
rooms, baroque piano, and kitchen floor tiles
courtesy of Leicester Cathedral; in stark contrast
is the heady bohemian vibe of Jimi Hendrix's digs
next door, with wild Carnaby prints, box TV and
a huge stack of cigarettes – as well as an original
guitar on which he played his blistering riffs. Revel
in the sedate surrounds where the famous *Messiah*
was composed, before advancing a few feet and
200 years to the crash pad of a rock 'n' roll legend.

25 Brook Street, Mayfair, W1K 4HB
Nearest station: Bond Street
Paid entry
handelhendrix.org

53

ATTENDANT

Spend more than a penny in a former public loo

Its above-ground presence is a jaw-dropping exploration in creative ironwork that you simply don't see in modern street furniture. This 130-year-old Victorian public convenience has been lovingly restored and repurposed as a sustainable coffee bar, where you are given a glimpse of oft-overlooked design history from a time when the humble lav was designed as thoroughly as a train station or hotel. The old toilet cistern is now a quirky planter trailing ivy, while the original Doulton urinals have been brilliantly reworked into individual spaces to perch and enjoy a top-notch dark roast or light bite. You'll leave feeling far more refreshed than those Victorian gents of old.

27a Foley Street, w1w 6dy
Nearest station: Oxford Circus, Goodge Street
the-attendant.com/pages/fitzrovia

54

LINLEY SAMBOURNE'S HOUSE

Historic home of a legendary illustrator

The home of the famed *Punch* magazine cartoonist is a time capsule of the 19th-century 'exotic' decor that was fashionable at the time. Despite the musty smell that greets you, it feels as though Sambourne has just popped out and will be back any moment, rather than having been dead since 1910. The chintzy, flocked-wallpaper rooms doubled as the workplace where he sketched. Don't miss the bathroom at the top of the house, where Sambourne developed photos that informed the poses of his caricatures, and the garden, which he used as a makeshift outdoor studio. In 1958 the Victorian Society was founded in the drawing room, pledging to preserve places like this for posterity.

18 Stafford Terrace, w8 7bh
Nearest station: High Street Kensington
Paid entry
rbkc.gov.uk/museums/sambourne-house

55

BERRY BROS. & RUDD

Historic wine merchant

This is one of the most prestigious wine merchants in the country, and while the shopfront is from the 19th century the business behind it dates back to 1698. Lord Byron, Prime Minister William Pitt and Beau Brummell all bought wine from here, and a certificate in the corner documents the loss of 69 cases of wine on the RMS *Titanic*. Inside, the decor feels little changed since those days, but this was the first independent wine merchant to install high-spec temperature controls to create optimum storage conditions. The cavernous, vaulted cellars extend beneath the shop and under adjacent Pickering Place (no.49) and Pall Mall, covering an area of two acres. These can be visited as part of tutored wine tasting events and private dining, which can be booked online.

63 Pall Mall, St James's, SW1Y 5HZ
Nearest station: Piccadilly Circus
bbr.com

IMAGE CREDITS

CONTRIBUTORS

Sheldon K. Goodman is a public historian and tour guide with over a decade of experience researching and exploring London's history. He is a lover of graveyards, LGBTQ+ history and historic pubs, and when not going down a research rabbit hole, writes for his blog Cemetery Club.

Hoxton Mini Press is a small indie publisher based in east London. We make books about London (and beyond) with a dedication to lovely, sustainable production and brilliant photography. When we started the company, people told us 'print was dead'; we wanted to prove them wrong. Books are no longer about information but objects in their own right: things to collect and own and inspire. We are an environmentally conscious publisher, committed to offsetting our carbon footprint. This book, for instance, is 100 per cent carbon compensated, with offset purchased from Stand for Trees.

INDEX

An Opinionated Guide to Historic London
First edition

Published in 2023 by Hoxton Mini Press, London
Copyright © Hoxton Mini Press 2023. All rights reserved.

Text by Sheldon K. Goodman
Copy-editing by Gaynor Sermon
Proofreading by Octavia Stocker
Design by Richard Mason
Production by Sarah-Louise Deazley
Production and editorial support by Georgia Williams

With thanks to Matthew Young for initial series design.

Please note: we recommend checking the websites listed for each
entry before you visit for the latest information on price, opening times
and pre-booking requirements.

A CIP catalogue record for this book is available from the British Library.

ISBN: 978-1-914314-46-9

Printed and bound by OZGraf, Poland

Hoxton Mini Press is an environmentally conscious publisher, committed
to offsetting our carbon footprint. This book is 100 per cent carbon
compensated, with offset purchased from Stand For Trees.

For every book you buy from our website, we plant a tree:
www.hoxtonminipress.com